D1356019

Montaigne's Tower and other poems

By the same author

Poems
Collected Poems 1963-1980
The Cornish Dancer
History of Him
Twists of the Way
The Fiesta
Angles and Circles
Sad Grave of an Imperial Mongoose
Penguin Modern Poets 23 (with Edwin Muir and Adrian Stokes)
Discoveries of Bones and Stones
Ingestion of Ice Cream
A Skull in Salop
Collected Poems 1924-1962
The Isles of Scilly
Under the Cliff
Several Observations

Celebration and Criticism
Recollections, mainly of Writers and Artists
The Private Art
Blessings, Kicks and Curses
The Goddess of Loving
Britain Observed
The Englishman's Flora
Notes from an Odd Country
The Contrary View
Poems and Poets

Anthologies
The Cherry Tree
The Oxford Book of Satirical Verse
Rainbows, Fleas and Flowers
The Faber Book of Reflective Verse
The Faber Book of Poems and Places
The Faber Book of Love Poems
The Faber Book of Popular Verse
The Faber Book of Nonsense Verse
The Penguin Book of Ballads
Unrespectable Verse

Montaigne's Tower and other poems

Geoffrey Grigson

Secker & Warburg
London

First published in England 1984 by
Martin Secker & Warburg Limited
54 Poland Street, London W1V 3DF

British Library Cataloguing in Publication Data

Grigson, Geoffrey
Montaigne's Tower and other poems.
I. Title
821'.914 PR6013.R744

ISBN 0-436-18806-6

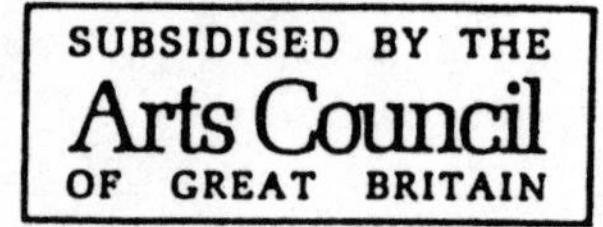

Printed in Great Britain by
Redwood Burn Limited
Trowbridge

For H. M. J. G.

Yet much can be grown
In good earth, alone,
In a world of stone.

Acknowledgements

Poems in this collection have appeared first in *Encounter,* the *Listener,* the *Literary Review,* the *London Magazine* and the *Times Literary Supplement.* Others are reprinted from the pamphlet *Twists of the Way* (Mandeville Press, 1980).

Contents

At Rokeby

I thought of that failed poet, irritating, puttyish, pale.
I thought, How many settled he unsettled by his cleverness.
I thought of his all self-cognizant pains and miseries.
I thought about his energies and ecstasies.
I thought, How these transcended all self-cognizance.
I thought, How, though itching with anxieties,
He rooted, here, in rock beside this polished water-rock.
I thought, How above this flow, above this water-slide,
He watched a final red leaf quiver on a winter tree.
I thought again, How this failure lives in his ecstasy.

Monkeys

i

Less monkeys than we were,
But monkeys still,
We've lost that lovely art
Of swaying along through trees.
We shave; perfect a more
Inclusive way to kill
And then excuse ourselves
By snivelling on our knees.

ii

But is that fair? They say
Gorillas couple face to face,
And while they couple, make
A noise like doves.
We should have much improved
Upon their loves.

Montaigne's Tower

Was it really here, in this tiled room
In this tower that Montaigne wrote?
I hope that it was so. Never was there
A place better for recalling, I would say –
For being benign and wise, for loving
In words. I see him back a chair
Across these tiles, and stand and stretch, and then
Descend this newel stair, and going
Slowly as if arthritically outside.
He looks down, with feeling he sees again
How exceedingly sweet is this meadowed
Small valley below and how half-reddening
Vines in such a light cast straight
Black bars of shadow in row after row.

A Bow to Rhyme

Rhyme bounces its cheques. Of course.
Rhyme's lost old friends. That's true,
But Rhyme's not entirely lost
Me, though it may have lost you.

Rhyme's ashamed, tightening up at the ends.
Inside Rhyme's hanging its head.
Rhyme's feeling a bit of a shit, I think
Rhyme's pretty near dead.

And look, D. Donoghue's there at the wake,
For Jasus' sake flogging the rye,
And not one of these creeps of the campus
Is wiping an eye.

Boy-O, I say to Rhyme, if you like,
Rhyme beginnings, middles and ends.
You don't need to say Sir,
You don't need all those old friends.

That's about it, I now say to Rhyme.
Tail up, Rhyme. And cheers.
True you may not be needed as heretofore,
But I judge you will be round for years.

You mayn't be a *sine qua non,* Rhyme.
But on rhymed beginning, middle and end,
Whatever these creeps insist, much
Good versing's still going to depend.

Degree Giving

Faced by the *Journal of Applied*
    Improbability in blue covers
(At which Chak Kong Kam, student from
    Malaysia, also was glancing)
I thought how many – would they say areas
    Or fields – of processes
Of mind are to most of us impenetrable.
    Later, bursts came from a Pseudo-Gothic
Organ over the Vice-Chancellor.
    Why at that moment – but
You can guess – did I think of Edward
    Chicken, parish clerk of
An inner parish of Newcastle-upon-Tyne
    And his poem about how
A collier and his doxy were joined
    In not such holy matrimony;
After which they snatched, in church,
    Garters off the thighs
Of the bride? And then pits once more
    Yawned very black and they
Pissed by blind ponies and glittering seams
    In their degree, diurnally.

Biography of a Militant

Young, in a brief circumference of flowers,
He did not know.
In middle age and still employed,
He did not dare,
And old,
He does not care.

Policy Statement

My brother's knapped a bright flint knife
I rather think to take my life.
That being so I've knapped another
So that I may kill my brother;
This policy we all agree
To tap out on our tomtom tree.

Indian Waitress in a Café

This piece of temple sculpture has detached herself:
She carries coffee to a customer.
To say she swans across would be quite wrong,
Quite foreign to her culture. Swans or swanning it
Are no part of temple sculpture.

Observe the way she undulates, the way she sways.
How differently her not pendulous breasts
Are attached to the top curve of her *S*-like
Undulation. You suppose she eagerly undulates
In brown sandstone only naked in the night? I'm

Sure you are right: carrying coffee to a customer
Does not count, though her flat backside clings
In a drooping firmness to her undulation.
I'm sure you are right: at night, in this cold
Climate of our northern culture, only in full

Active undulation does she leap with lovers
To rejoin brown sandstone temple sculpture.

First Glimpse of the Auvergne Volcanoes

Forgetting that to some degree, e.g.,
We are both classics and romantics,
Also that history's mood and mode
Insist on differences of code,
To straighten up our soppier antics
We take to structure and semantics.
  Not to indulge in finding Beauty
Became years ago a solemn duty,
But having reached this *point de vue,*
Wouldn't it be a faker's pose,
Against this sky of rose,
To underplay these peaks of blue?

For the Living

A litany for the Living;
  From pain, pestilence, and automatic rifles,
  From inconsolable ache,
  From the empty bed,
  From hardness of heart and contempt
    For the poor muddled head,

And no requiem, none at all,
For those who are dead.

The Cold Photo

White clouds move into blue
Over our cliff, light sparkles on trees below.
Only now and again, though, we are out of the wood,
And kissing a photograph is a cold
Business, and does little good.

Picnic Place in October

This great chestnut tree suggests in mid
October, noble so sheerly in its kind,
A live head of a father of gods, his slightly
Swaying locks making him seem so much more benign.

Or it might be not dissimilar grand
Poseidon's head thrust out of blue
Into blue, his damp locks, drying, in this
Slight breeze swaying too.

Descendants of this or that great tree,
Greece not forgotten, may suggest such
To descendants of ourselves, if by ourselves
Is allowed of our present world this much,

If great gods resembling and suggested
By great sweet chestnut trees continue so,
If much longer by ourselves permitted,
Great trees in this noble way sway to and fro.

Land's End

It seems most of us stood here once
With some indifference, on this last rock
Named Finis Terrae. Deep steep down-hills
And climbs, slow green surges-forward swelled

And thumped below, arriving from somewhere
Unknown about which we did not care.
Metaphysically might a few speak of these
Surgings-forward as if adjunct to defined

Permitted mystery. Whales might
Know more, whales also did not care.
So we turned our sheep-skinned backs to
That incessant wind off-sea, our face to what

We knew by land. Among such were screams of
Pleasures of our appetites, screams of delivery,
Screams of wounds in war, high long
Pitch of Haydn's violins, sonnets

Again read, countings of cash, quick
Graces public and intimate, feel of hands.
Of the rapt few, have some since – no wonder –
Thrown their silvered images away,

Sceptical of belief, there's now nothing
They can't quickly turn up or verify about
Let's say great waves and surges. We have
Pictures of very far away small

Pools and lakes and capes, measurements too
Of seas we do not visit. We have maps,
And instancy. Ignorant as we may be
Of ourselves, and sceptical of glory,

Most of us are still not much concerned
By ends in earth awaiting us, or even ends,
As once before vaguely we supposed
Must come to us, by staggering fire.

Atlantic Evening

Everything which is, which ever was, which ever
Will be good, absolutely is at times confirmed.

It rains, too, coldly hours on end, is sullen. Everything
Is dark, is smudged, everything confirms our
Misery, which, inter-set, equally endures, returns,
Everlastingly, I mean, occurs, recurs,
Equally.

Now listen as you need to do, to long, low, slow waves,
To faint warm audibilities of air, long thin fadings
Of scented tones of colours vanishing.
Look also how as ever beyond stripped sands, glitterings
Of silver also as ever add to blue;

Only a few walk on these wet new sands.

Swallows at Sparrowthorn

Watching late in June earth's green hair
Lazily tossed by intermittent winds
In sunshine, after rain,
I say inevitable pleasure again
Drives out inevitable pain.

So we talked yesterday, on Cotswold,
Three writers and three wives.
And there were children to be fetched
From school, and these would soon
Be flown; and I considered

How our hosting family, through the timbers
Of their covered alley the parent
Swallows flying without fear,
Momentarily were blessed
By having their first swallows' nest.

Thank You

You tell us what art ought to do,
How it should be pick-me-up and pills.
But then being Us, from our delight,
Distress, disharmony, dismay,
Our words insist on saying what they say.

Epitaph

Götterdämmerung – quite right.
And then they died. Then
Blackness of a yawning
Vacuum.
Now in his span he saw
Fancied Almightiness transformed to real,
His fellows, in two parties,
Becoming genuine Lords of Hell,
And in dismay he tolled
His funeral bell.

Soap Operations

Have they moved, I wonder, their slaughter house
From the easy view of all who bring them
Oodles of money? In this coloured ad
For their ancient once very wealthy small
Mercantile city I detect no purple
Water, of blue and of blood drained out of
Bullocks. I see no angler with a flower
In his mouth perched over that heretofore
Purple. Of course bullocks' blood would be
No right sacrifice for their present god
In this now communist tourist city.
Like most of us I think they live mostly
Out of cans of Argentine beef. And soon
Will not such wine as they drink and offer
Their tourists come all the way from that
Napper Valley, conveyed all that way
To what for various reasons was called once
The Wine Dark Sea? Sveti Vlaho, whom we know
As Saint Blaise, Protector of Woolcombers,
Still looks from his niche in this charming
City's surrounding sea-wall. Except from
A boat he is not easily seen. You ask,
Should he not be removed and replaced with
A strong bearded Marx interpreted wrongly
Or a Red Star at night brightly lit up?
It's true monks patter on sun-heated stone,
But are they not part of that décor, part
Of that soap opera, provided not
Altogether with cynicism, helping
To pay for that corned grief in cans?
  Glaring white is their cruise boat on blue,
From which sounds a hoot. Camera cases
Bump on behinds. Hurry aboard. Embark,
My dears, for your life's next island illusions.

26

Song
(from the Portuguese of Fernando Pessoa)

Are elves or sylvans playing?
These rhythms of music, these shades
Of sound, these breathings among pines
Float round; or are like curves in roads

From places never known to me? They
Are like someone disappearing, then
Appearing among trunks of trees. Echoing
Something far away which never

Can be mine, these faint sounds – yet why? –
Bring me almost to tears,
This tune so tenuous I ask if it
Is real? Or no more than a sadness

Of evening, me, and pines? It dies
And like a breeze losing its
Shape of sighs, is once more
Only a rustling through the trees.

Empty Purse Mill

Scraggily stood my miller, dust
Floated out of his half-hatch door,
Hens pecked round the holes which his rats
Had bitten out of the floor.

Empty Purse was the name of that mill.
Never its miller was well-to-do.
The manor it served was too small,
Its tied tenants were far too few.

Here was the finish of centuries, here
Mud slowly silted his pool,
And his son deserted to Canada
After calling his father a fool.

Rumble O, rumble O, went that wheel
With such failing business to tell,
And to eels under figwort and brambles
The leakings of water fell.

Before he vamoosed overseas, with one
Change of old clothes and no more,
That son of my miller re-nailed
An empty purse over the door.

And What Then?

Like a dove's, a mottled hawk's breast is sweet,
A hawk high up, on a dead wrist of a tree, waiting
With a taxidermist's bright eye,
For the least life below,
Which it will rip into foul strips, and eat.
Like a dove's, a hawk's breast is sweet.

Habitat

We are that rock in whose clefts and holes
Pitiless hobs and sharp goblins dwell –
That being the verb we used, to dwell, in
Times when we believed in Hell.
And outside, in our limestone dell,
Do grow rare lilies of the valley and ivory
Orchids, which sweetly smell.

No Longer

No longer, he said, for me
Does a red flower open in a black tree.
And look at him there, among tattered
Prayer-books, down on his knee.

On the Sideboard

Stands by odd accident upon our medieval
Virgin's head a postcard of Matisse's somewhat
Abstract very naked girl in blue. That's

Blasphemous to you? But then our blasphemies
Are not all or not at all the same? Might it not be
A blasphemy for me if – our sideboard differently arranged –

Our Virgin Mary's stony feet trod on Matisse's naked
Blue? Our limestone Virgin in another way is
Abstract too – a different abstract maybe

Of the true, if not to me? Perhaps in one
Image of the mind we might effect – *Ave Maria,*
Plena gratiae, ex tacta et intacta Virgine –

A reconciliation of the two? Or after all,
Are not another way, of him and her, both *blasphemous*
And *worshipful* now irremediably *vieux jeu?*

House of Art

Betraying that soft Bloomsbury kink,
Even piano legs inside this restless House
Of Art in slack wide strokes were
Spiralled blue and pink;

Which made piano music sound no sweeter.
Outside rose midges from a stagnant ditch
That by a long chalk was no
Cotman's sparkling Greta.

They added this soft sentiment of pink and blue
To cosy them from existential stink.
Now – five shillings to go in – it's hoped
This house will do as much for me and you.

Villon

How is it, unlike most, that Villon
Could come clean,
Could stay clean; tender, living,
Lyrically, amusedly obscene?

Not like others who cosied
Themselves in furcoats of their time?
Keeping up with Jones the God
And with Jones the Poet
Did them in. Villon lives, you might
Say, naked in rhyme.

April Values

  Let us sing
Of Literary Values
  In the Spring.

Though as always many things
Are far from well,
Though we find ourselves propelled
Down some new avenue to hell;
Though loud Burgess reads us
Lectures on Malayalam
And similar manufacturers continue
Pumping water into ham
And strawberries are rather few
In full-fruit strawberry jam,
Let us not prefer
Ashbery to Yeats,
Let us not suppose T. Hughes,
On shining floors,
Goes waltzing with a lyrical Muse.
Let's not confuse
Swallows in these April skies
With awkward rooks,
Or profess ourselves impressed
By some new amateur
Review of Books;
Let's confess
Poetry is in its usual mess;
Let's not be, like
Tiddlywinks, abusive,
Only this new season
All the more
Exclusive.

After a Revealing Biography

Once tickled pink to have been in it,
Now it seems that every minute
One more survivor of the dead
Shuffles embarrassed from his bed.

Sunday Editor

Everything about him is a lie
Including (on T.V.) that twinkle
In his abominable alcoholic eye.
He lies to himself as much, Sabbath
By Sabbath, as he lies to those poor bleeders
He calls his "faithful readers".

A History of Literature

I tell you what he wrote – then crumpled up:
        "Doves do not come until all
        Trees are leaved.
        Love may speak, and
        Yet may not be seen."
What are the rhymes for leaved?
A damp wind blurred the stagnant
Water of the treeless fen.
That crumpled paper floated away,
And he became the loneliest of men.

Joseph Haydn

I remember little of things
Which I see on the screen,
But once, Joseph Haydn,
In a mass after midnight
I saw stone rays spreading
Out from your name, I supposed
It was over your grave. Also
A woman kneeling, who sang
Your music, alone,
In a dark nave.

Execution Place in the Mountains

This place, this stone court round a cross
Is not evil at all. This locked little church
Isn't powerful at all. In trucks evil rolled up.
Evil pocked the soft stone of this wall.

Where Adam and Rachel play in sunshine
Today did evil see how this brook bubbled,
How extra green the grass was, where warm bodies
With tied wrists shuddered and doubled?

Did evil remark how extra yolk-yellow kingcups
Were marking the flow – not so long ago?
Now I observe that as well in the lushness hiding the flow
Many delicate not quite so yellow wild tulips blow.

A Late Summer

It begins with gout, it goes on
With veins, then a touch of arthritis.
It continues with blue pillules
For the heart to pump smoothly.

Pissing then plays you
Up. They cut into you, and at last
You are told that cells which may
or may not be "controllable",
Are insisting on independence.

Revolution in the body-republic.

Is it surprising after so many
Years that your intermittency
Of visiting doctors does not any
More continue in confidence?
That the bonhomie which set
You up, is reduced now to
Quietly sober revelation, and
Instruction? And that over
Coffee you stare at the infants,
At some especial only balding
Thinness, and regard those
Who are not, fortunately, old?

That you ask your sad
Self what you have done? What
You have made? What pleasure
You have given to those whom
You do not know? That you in dismay,
Not yet – if soon – in despair,
Prefer to remember blue hills
In ranks under rose clouds

In blue? How you sat on yellow
Bales in picnic, together, and
Stared at this floating of rose
In a windless blue, as if there for ever?
Sticking, after, that photo alone
On one page in your album?

Edward Thomas

This violin poet did not raise his voice.
He was unhappy in circumstance and choice,
Yet he was a poet able to rejoice.

B.N.

How he set circles among skewed angles, how
Through life he recalled surfaces and sand-islands
Creating plane on top of plane along that low
Sinuous reflective river of France which though
It might rise to a beastly power, for him always
Contra-indicated disharmony and strain.

Then, in extreme age, no longer travelling so far
How, from his low sports car, in the rain, along the sinuous
Wharfs he drew in firmest lines a like equanimity again.

On a Picture Sold with Regret

That bright face of pink-over-blue in that hand of cards
Dealt on to stripes of earth-brown and cloud-grey –
How it scores high, that hand! How, recollected uncolourful
Day after day, that order of colours drives ennui away!

Art Gallery Window

Looking through this white art gallery's
Window I see past framed fisty pinkest
Blossoms of may slowly shooting criss-crossing
Portions of a great fountain, wavering,
Falling, frailly, to lake water blue but
As well reflecting brown. Children in red
Run by between blue water and pink may.
I do not say nature is superior etcetera
To art, only that on such a morning as in this
Northern city there is also to be practised
An art of looking steadily outward through
Windows of galleries of art.

Bergen

After the Plane

New:
A sinuous pink oleander
On the lapping blue.

Alive

Accuse me of making a list.
Very well, I make such a list: I say
  That at stepping-stones tide
  Reverses the flow, samlets
  Are silvered, flags clatter. Fruits
  Hang dull black from alders.
  Faggots are chopped for firing.
  Mist has gone, smoke is rising.

Sneer I am making a list.
I am, and my list continues.
  That most minute flower named
  After Sibthorpe who by Flaxman
  Steps in Greek costume ashore
  To number flowers of Greece
  And of Crete, trails in a corner –
  There, where a mossed rock is dribbling.

Buzzards mew. A fisherman now
Jerks a Blue Upright from figwort.
  Upstream brambles are hiding
  A holy well. Here occurs bog-myrtle
  Fragrance; upstream, osmunda.
  Here stand thin oaks for rinding;
  Upstream hill shafts descend
  to long-flooded alleys

Of silver and mundic. And my
List continues, beyond concept
  And words. Beyond books are
  This stream and these hills.
  Here do gates sag, do no spiked
  Wires intercept, does property
  Seem not asserted. And my old
  List is alive; and continues.

Creature Misnamed

A species of elegance is that Gray Wagtail,
Who is yolk-yellow, who is not gray, who wiggles
An extra-long, narrow tail, who steps with delicacy,
Who in a flutter after flying food does appear frail.

I like this bird, who lives in corners which are green,
Rocky, secret and wet, who has no common
Or robinish fame; which does not matter one gnat
To that whether-or-no-egg-yellow species I mean.

Exactly

Exactly:
Along with a gaggle of geese, etc.,
A merde of writers is the apt collective term
For those soft furry and so cuddly writers who
In every book, book-nook and book review,
Make seemliness of letters squirm –
Or you might call them that always-with-us crew
Of Dwarf Panders, avid for bamboo.

Memorial

You can sit on this author here in the sun
Since his ashes were mixed with cement and sand
Into this block which weighs a ton,
Out in this far away cactus land.

Barely Enough

With what lack of coyness my colleagues
Now write of the feminine bush.
In flats they set birds on a bed
And bushiness goes to their head.

Breasts out of bras are old hat, so they're
Off over downlands and dunes to where
The garrigues more scented and lush,
With a whiff of salt in the air.

It's not that I avidly care for lyrics
Of skylark and thrush, it's not
That I don't care for bodies, and don't
Like them decidedly bare, without

In most areas hair. But don't tell me
That ultimate pleasures were not more keen
When magistrates cried "obscene!"
And pubics were skirted with stiff bombazine.

Twists of the Way

If we could we would, yet where?
Luck deflects us, watching
Scarlet among trees, or through their grille
Brown monks S-curving

To their knees. We take the deviation,
By the flattened hedgehog on the lane,
Cross the allegoric ford Distress,
And for a while admire

The play of Corot's green and grey
Around the hamlet Happiness. Then
A drift of rain or pain alters
The way we meant again.

Incommunicando

He says "Our hearts are incommunicando" –
Whether we will communicate our hearts
Or no, even to ourselves. I used not
To think this could be so; only, I thought,
I was afraid to see and estimate
What usage calls a heart – my heart in me.
  I write. Yet who is I or Me? I thought –
Still like to think – to write alone
Is to be free. My daughter writes from far
Away and signs her letter "Love
From Me". Who is this other Me? Who's Me,
This other Me she writes to? Who,
Peeled to the heart, I ask again, is She?

He Should Have Said

Here I recall a sky, he said, of breezeless
Blue on which hung berries of enamelled red.
Also across a green morass a pony's long,
Hollow-eyed, bleached head.
And nothing else?
Answering that half tender, half ironic
Whisper from the dead, I remember most
The expections of that brilliant day,
He should have said.

Comfort to Come

She wakes up: nightingales and incessant
River outside; and he is there, yes, there alive;
And asleep, in depth asleep, so his breathing
Denotes, by her side, and she cries.

He goes on breathing aloud. Not a stir, but
he hears how she cries. Better, he thinks, if two
Years or so had already slipped by since he died,
And comfort had come; and he sleeps,

And she cries, now with hardly a cry
He could hear, warm and still the length of her side.
Now again in his dream he is at home and a child.
Now awake, still awake, she is afraid; and she cries.

A Change of View

It's changed. High exasperated cliffs,
Also high rough rocks, preferred, preferred,
Prevented a right liaison with that
Sea. I looked down at its breaking

Heave, for clearer view I crossed
And crossed again small streams
Sidling in cliff dells through
Hummocks of sedge. These leapt, but

Turned to spray, dwindling toward sea-spray
Below. By these cliff-trickles
Orchid-masts transmitted purple-blue
And so far down below shags drove

With purpose out and in across
Important heaves of the sea. Ravens
Sounded a deep nasal N and K.
And now it's changed.

Now give me for at least
A simulacrum of a union with the sea,
To be, without others, on a rare wild,
Slight-shelving and warm-sanded

Infinite strand where airs of the sea
Encounter a land breeze from low
Pines; where flows in, millimetres
Deep, high tide in whispering

Curls and curves, each expunging more,
And then more fine inscriptions
Left by pied waders quickly running
Delicate feet along this now engaged,

Sadly and softly marriageable sea,
And how out on the cool low generous
Bay glimmer flower-colours of yet
Unvisited desirable islands the whole day.

Good

The slopes of this world
Are huge. Cold mists covering
Them are shifted by the sun,
And the mille-fleur has begun.

In the Zoo

What culture will this ape-child inherit
In his white hygienic age? His mother
Shields him with a tender arm, she eats
His afterbirth; and he relaxes, held
To her enormous hairy breast, and is
Briefly and dreamlessly at rest, closing
Such babyish ancient anxious wrinkled eyes.

Watch his huge male parent next, watch
His weary muscular four-legged walk
To nothing at all across his white hygienic
Cage. Watch his immense felted thighs, when his
Ancient apishness is smudged, and slowly,
Dully, his leafaged dream of ape-life dies.

Old Folks' Outing

Sceptics, watching Gascons
With enormous noses
Paying francs to stare
At wonder-carvings in this
Famous choir,
May well enquire

Just who God thinks he is
To exact as here marble
And gilded oak from man
In thanks or fear –

And then who shuffling
Gascon peasants
With long noses
Think they are
That God might care.

Wild Garden

My Preface to Your Unfashionable Collected Poems

Entering your wild Gothic at this high gate,
Where entry's gratis and plan and guide
To a strange nomenclature come free, no need that I

Should doubt which way to go. Once past
This natural arch I choose this way below
Thick leaves where hiding birds sing *loriot* –

This path dipping to springs which spread and vein
Sparse moss on slabbed limestone, and drip and drip;
From clefts, here, poise in wet air blue petals

Of hepatica fringing their white-stitched
Circle-centres of an acidic green,
Over smooth lobes of kidney-leaves in threes.

You are – old in wilderness, I say;
Purpose in wildness, then surprise. You are
Stack and spike. You are shelf, cave, depth, twist, cool;

Auricular hollow, obstacle, light;
Black, grey, secret and absolution;
And solution, as if this pine, as Chinese

Among rocks drew a single pine. Newly
I am compelled to your sky-height, again
Your utmost up in air; to balance there

By rust and magenta of low alpen-
Rose, where bilberries too mat that hard long
Rib of rock – across grand hollowness

To stare, to stare and stare at most art-struck small
Dead volcanoes, acting eternities
In those hepaticas' same sweet sharp blue.

Cor Cordium

On what level floated what was called
The soul? It floated, I would say, in middle air
Not here, not there, not caught in nets,
Succumbing not to stone from slings or shot,
Hymns from it sidling like savour of burned
Bones and flesh and fat to the god's ear.

Going deep, and deeper, down to what we'd say
Is heart we must prefer.

Where Are You?

Snow, snow through grey air
Outside this window.
Snow over this glum sea, low,
Driving in. Snow covers
That hard to discover sea-pink
Settee, on which love was free.
Snow, how many despondently say,
Wavers between you and me.
Snow overflows that once
Warm breast-cup woven
Into our black-twigged
Gateway tree.

Wild Threshing Olive Trees

Left to yourselves, not tutored to a fork
For bettering your fruit, splitting,
Twisting, minus snakes you are Laocoön;
And down these steeps November stormings

Flash you white, now lash you white.
And worse, they'll come and beat you
With long sticks, your olives pattering
To black glistening sheets.

In March cyclamens will open
Between the scarred writhings of your feet.

At the Zinc Counter

A black glass in our hand,
Yellow scum on this black liquor.
Half empty now. What worth is that
Old Sow which eats her farrow?

Sea crinkles in, but then streaks
Out and out. What else can that
Old Sow do? Here are we
Pushed to our limit

Of land. And suppose we cross
This outstreaking extra sea, we find
What, but another unsatisfactory,
Unsatisfying land, where again we lie

In not our ancient soil,
But where embalmed we shall be
With that fixed wax smile, or burned.
Not even this blown sand are we.

Boats

Poems and boats have this in common:
They had better float.
Engines they do not entirely need,
Dismountable, transferable, outboard.

Oars will do; or anchors
After all, anchoring so that
Poems and boats instead of still,
Pulse lightly to a pulse

Of passing water, lapping,
Lively. If they float it's
All the same whether or no poem
Or boat is given a name.

Few boats are gilt barges of occasion.
Some are gondolas, a little fake
Also. Some, Old Rusty Rails, are vulgar
Ferries; more, white dip-dipping

Yachts directed by off-duty
Dentists. Most are prams
Which nip like limericks. And as well
There are folded neatly paper boats.

These quickly suck up water
When they are set afloat.
Better – for poets – not to be
Captain, or cargo, of a paper boat.

He Has Passed Over

You can't say his white soul flits round
This atmosphere of ours in a state of grace.
Perhaps it wobbles round, lacking
Pegasus-power to push into space.
And if it had enough Pegasus-power,
What would it find there
But a further extension of the commonplace?

What Goes to Which?

So they leave him to burn.
Tomorrow in his own car
They will bring him back home in a tasteful urn.
Then they will get down to dividing the spoils,
Shares, antique silver, Constable sketches and oils.

It's down on paper, dears, what goes to which;
All the same, dears, you know our steppy's a bitch.
What has she salted away in her room?
In that secret drawer, behind that locked door –
As if we can't guess?

What she hides away from your sneer,
In a secret drawer, behind a double-locked door
Is how she felt in his arms,
And her emptiness.

Our Village Once

His Lord awarded him this Cornish land.
Breton he spoke. Which was to speak much as
His serfs spoke after all. Yet Breton or no
I can't suppose their new boss soothed them
With a light, or extra loving hand.

What's left of him? No gallows now. Only
A sunk track to his hall (which now we call
Hall Farm) – a timber job, hearth in the middle;
Above the mean, and far below the grand.

What would he recognize? Not much. It was
His grandson built that rebuilt church. Perhaps
He might be pleased to see – with cattle around –
That dancing spring lifting bright domes of sand.

In his day – but now who keeps a pig? – blood
For black puddings spirted by this spring, pigs'
Carcases were scalded and then shaved, just there
Where our three menhir-pumps for petrol stand,

And tripes they washed, grey yards and yards of tripes
Uncoiled and flushed, bits floating off to eels
Which lurked in ugly mud downstream. Here stank
An oak-pit too where dark pigs' skins were tanned.

That's all I shall recall. I fancy, though,
Our Breton Lord's dull skull, lacking no more
Than a hollow tooth or two, lies lapped,
In comfort still, below his stolen land.

August

In that grand house lost in tall stands
Of Sweet Corn down a gravelly track
They are playing bridge, in peace.
A head of Buddha, bought in Paris, watches them.
Dummy gets up to let some new guests in.
Three no trumps are won; and now the chatter
Following the sacred silence seems a different matter.

Birthday

An old Coade Stone head
On a no longer attended-to
Rockery, behind grass and ferns?

Well, they have their own concerns,
And what they say is, tactfully,
Happy Birthday today, not
Many Happy Returns.

Ignorance

Contemplating in its blue cover the *Journal*
Of Applied Improbability and realizing
There exist areas of activity
Of the mind for ever unfamiliar to most of us
I leave humbly this university building
In search of a pissoir.

Rats

Raised (we think) above grey rats, how we remain
Rattier than rats, and yet discriminate;
And if rats love (as we love), be sure if rats fear
And so at times kill their mates, rats do not hate.

O Fair Aurelia

This was not drudgery in Aurelia's womb.
She worked it wonderfully and I lay back
Amazed. Blue-eyed she was, and I
With my dog's teeth in her shoulder
Had supposed her old and dry,
And now I lay back drained.
Living's grim force insisted, beyond rhyme,
And I'm admitting, weakly, I was framed.

Quid Pro Quo

Seduced by scented May along the rides,
Into the fall-trap he had dug he fell,
Where frightened beasts jumped at the steep sides,
Then turned and tore each other and himself as well.

Incident

Seven eyes of wavering blue confront you
When they turn round, father, mother,
Girl and son. Take care. When I jumped off
My ferny wet stone hedge to stammer
My respects, my act was not well taken.
At once the pallid one-eyed son
Felled me with a bloody brainy hammer.

Elegy for Extra-Homes

Shabbier grow loved extra-homes, though a new
Arrived dove behind hawthorn flowers crools now,
Now crools again, now again, on first-coming days
Which are grey – if with a blue patch or two, still

Grey, still grey. Paint's worn from woodwork away.
Rust. Now not one key turns easy. Not as quickly,
Now holiday's come, are shrubs cut to comfort, gravels
Chemically weeded, whole gardens to rights set more

Or less. But each owner's older: he may – does he know it? –
Soon be sentenced to die. Habit his life is.
His children – their children – come now no more.
He cleans up. A bonfire. Pink puppets – fire eats

Their features. And cleavers, how insistently cleavers
Climbs in all corners. He's been cut into. He can lift
Nothing. She must lift all. He sleeps after eating. Hell,
Sole Hell he fears now, is horrible dying, asking, asking

Well, was it worth it? "It" is that consequential, oddest
Of accidents. "It" equals living, is all he recalls,
All he's forgotten. Who said to him in his schooling:
Make bad less bad for man, if you can. Make good

More good for man, if you can? Who said: In absurdity
Soothe. Soothe, soothe, if you can – as soothed you
Have been? Who said, That is most, though it may not be
All, we being deceivers, in being a man.

At Colmar, in June, outside the Museum

Should I like to be one whose
Present expenditure of breath
Might bend gleaming summer
Grasses of a future time,
Sounding for some lives, for a while,
As others have sounded for mine,
A gently resonant comforting chime,
Carrying as well a scent of lime?

Quae nunc abibis in loca
Pallidula, rigida, nudula

"The City of Memories", complex
Of recollections of half-desires
And evasions, of peopled alleys,
But also of grand empty avenues
Leading to shabby sentries in scarlet –

Escaping from occasion of memories
To another azure horizon which
Is edged by nothing, I come
By an ochre lane to a now nearly
Unpeopled river, where mill-wheels

Sag, cross by timber over a weir's
White noise, enter a darkness now not
Soft with flour, under still millstones
Over beams upheld by oak pillars
Reminiscent vaguely of Rome.

All around either white agitation
Or stillness of water. In one corner
Campari and whisky, in another
Red glow of flameless logs
And a low large bed for two.

Of these two, one sits outside
On this island. His large-leaved Paulownia
Shades him. He is holding a rod,
But is nearly asleep. Only this foreign
Abandoned river is insistently flowing.

Death of a Rich Scholarly Bachelor

The principle of continuity
Will not, I realize, mourn
At his cremation, as the organ
Extones certainly
Abide with Me.

He abode with no one,
He was in love only
With that principle of going on:
He saved – it was his wife,
It was his family –

A medieval foundation:
Through him – but it will not
Attend his cremation – it
Will continue. In its
Quadrangle next week

You may touch unawarely
Of course a fragment of his
Scattered ashes. I myself, yes,
It is mean, but they would
Be meaningless, have

Sent no red roses. But
I look at his face, a corbel
Cut on his library, a cold stone
Face. And if he could persist
Outside appearances

With whom could he now be
Abiding, except continuity?
His stone face parodies him, who
Parodied living, though, I suspect,
Through no fault of his own.

Ecological Note

A daft cuckoo sings for other
Daft cuckoos into the dark.
An old-fashioned lark sings
In the high light to lazy
Larks still below in the dark.
No mouse squeaks to other mice
In this high-rise wall,
High concrete and steel allowing
No mouse-life at all.